BORROWED SPACE

First published in 2014 by
The Dedalus Press
13 Moyclare Road
Baldoyle
Dublin 13
Ireland

www.dedaluspress.com

Dedalus Press titles are represented in the UK by
Central Books, 99 Wallis Road, London E9 5LN
and in North America by Syracuse University Press, Inc.,
621 Skytop Road, Suite 110, Syracuse, New York 13244.

Printed in Ireland by Gemini International Ltd.

Cover image: 'Sophie' by Mark Granier,
courtesy of the photographer

The Dedalus Press receives financial assistance from
The Arts Council / An Chomhairle Ealaíon

BORROWED SPACE

New and Selected Poems

Enda Wyley

Introduction by

James L. Pethica

DEDALUS PRESS
DUBLIN, IRELAND

ACKNOWLEDGEMENTS

Acknowledgements are due to the editors of the following in which a number of my new poems have originally appeared: *Poetry Ireland Review, Shine On: Irish Writers for Shine* (ed. Pat Boran, Dedalus Press, 2012), *Windows 20 Publication, Cyphers, The Lighter Craft: A Festchrift for Peter Denman, The Stony Thursday Book, The Irish Times.*

Thank you to Clíodhna Ní Anluain for broadcasting over the years several of these poems on *Sunday Miscellany,* RTÉ Radio 1. 'Lost Angels' was written for the anthology and exhibition *Lines of Vision / Writers on Art* that forms a highlight of the National Gallery of Ireland's 150th Anniversary programme, 2014. Many thanks to Janet McLean and Marie Bourke, NGI.

The author is indebted to The Arts Council/ An Comhairle Ealaíon for a Bursary in Literature received in 2012, and a Patrick Kavanagh Fellowship which assisted in the completion of new poems for this book and the selection and editing of poems gathered here from four previous collections.

Many thanks to Prof. James L. Pethica, Williams College, USA, for his kind introduction to this volume; thanks too to the poet Thomas Lynch for his immediate and positive response; to Mark Granier for his cover photograph; to Catriona Dooley, Jenny McCrohan, Jacinta Wright, Anna Rowan and Lorraine Egan for their ongoing support. Dennis O'Driscoll first suggested the idea of this New and Selected — in memory and thanks. And to Freya and Peter Sirr with love.

Contents

≈

Introduction / 11

≈

from EATING BABY JESUS (1993)

Wedding Gift / 21
The Obstacle / 22
Orpheus Speaks / 23
Poems Whispered in Leningrad, 1940 / 24
Mandelstam / 25
Home from Sydney / 26
Eating Baby Jesus / 28
Where Poems Begin / 30
Books / 31
Measuring / 33
Cúil Aodha Singer / 37
Venus de Milo / 39
The Waitress has Transformed / 40
Wedding Bed / 41
Love Goes Home / 43
Municipal Gallery Favourite / 44
Swimmer / 46
Fall / 47
Triangle Path / 49
A Life / 51

from SOCRATES IN THE GARDEN (1998)

Mother / 55
Journey / 56
Socrates in the Garden / 59
Litany for a Sunny Day / 63
Magpie / 65
Ghosts / 67
Love Bruise / 70
Eight Short Love Poems / 71
Talking to the Bees / 76
Sean-Nós Singer / / 78
Hair / 80
Places You Have Found Me / 82
Five Definitions of a Butterfly / 85
The Soul Kisses Goodbye / 87

from POEMS FOR BREAKFAST (2004)

Dish of a Moon / 91
Two Women in Kosovo / 92
Cutting Hair on New Year's Day / 94
On My Father's Birthday / 96
Marlborough Road / 98
Poems for Breakfast / 100
Mint Gatherers / 101
Snorkelling with you / 102
St Patrick's Day / 104
Master Chef / 106
Emperor / 107
Short Love Poems / 108
Painter at Work / 110
At Work / 112

Diary of a Fat Man / 113
Walking with an Architect / 115
Somebody Has Died Close By / 117

from To Wake to This (2009)
Little Heart / 121
Twelve Days / 122
Bird / 123
To Wake to This / 125
Lucky / 126
Clooncunny / 127
Gold Wallpaper / 128
Sea Urchin / 130
Postcard / 131
Strange Things in Strange Places / 132
Notebook Shop / 133
The Page Within / 134
Night Guard / 135
Magpie / 137
Game / 138
Trees that Lead to You / 139
First Words / 140
War / 141
Blessing / 142
Postcards / 144

New Poems

Borrowed Space / 147
Gardens, Royal Hospital Kilmainham / 149
Poet / 150
Species / 151

Unveiling / 152
Julius Caesar had a Pet Giraffe / 154
Derrynane / 155
Letter in Winter / 158
Escaping the City / 159
Unbearable / 162
The Tao of Travel / 163
Rue Soufflot / 165
Lost Angels / 166
The News from Here ... / 168

For my mother, with love

*You, keeping me from the shabby coldness
of this outside world,
put the last stitch on my coat.*

Introduction

ENDA WYLEY REALISED early in life that she wanted to write. After first appearing in print as a young teenager, she was fortunate enough to receive crucial encouragement from established poets and critics and firmly announced herself in the 1990s as a distinctive new voice in Irish poetry. Taking stock of more than two decades of work, *Borrowed Space* comprises selections from her four collections published since 1993, along with new poems written since 2009. It offers us both a retrospective — a compressed and intensified accounting of Wyley's accomplishment to date — and, in the new poems, the forward-looking soundings and negotiations of a writer whose sense of the possibilities of poetry remains vital and immediate.

In *Eating Baby Jesus*, her debut volume with its attention-demanding title, Wyley's concern with the value and functions of poetry, literary craft and imagination was already sophisticated and assured. The lyrics in this volume repeatedly attend to the conditions that have always most made poetry necessary: loss, whether actual or anticipated; the desire for some kind of compensatory recovery; constriction or difficulty, whether personal, political or, in the process of writing, in the challenges of form and language itself; and an awareness of the past and its shaping influence on individual possibility. Wyley tellingly chose to open the volume (and now this collection) with a villanelle— a form in which the tightly-defined requirements of stanzaic pattern and repeated end-rhymes challenge a poet to find ways to be true to their own voice while also submitting to the discipline and constraints of tradition. 'Wedding Gift' indeed constitutes a young writer's manifesto. In imagining the dying Raymond Carver thinking of Chekhov's last months, it squarely acknowledges drawing inspiration from the achievements of past writers. Cavafy, Akhmatova, Larkin, Lowell, Mandelstam and others are named and conversed with as felt presences in the collection, and as exemplars of how one might "sing" in the face of oppression, loss or uncertainty. But in its images of leaping salmon as they "bend ecstatic" and "tussle free from the river" 'Wedding Gift' also asserts Wyley's desire to "map new routes" in her own art. The question of how and where to belong repercusses centrally throughout — *"Cad as duit?"* ("Where are you from?") she is pointedly asked in 'Cúil Aodha Singer' — amidst repeated reflections on the danger as well as the allure of being rooted tightly within a particular place, history or tradition. The collection closes with poems which hark back to her childhood holidays at Bundoran and which allude to starting a new life in Dublin after time spent abroad; and Yeats, that pre-eminent singer of uncertainty, is evoked here in 'Municipal Gallery Favourite'.

But this return home is pointedly figured as being modified and enriched by what has been brought from the world beyond those Irish origins. In 'A Life', Wyley describes tracing a circle in the head of pint of Guinness with a dip of Cointreau. The action creates an unexpected "mix" and causes the conversation of the person who drinks it to "expand" beyond what is socially "safe" after they have downed several glasses. New route and existing river of tradition are figuratively blended here, bringing about an intoxication which is imaginatively liberating but also recognised as potentially dangerous or undisciplined.

This first collection features much conscious self-positioning of the kind necessary for any young artist. But these early poems are well aware that others' writings can only be a starting point, and they make their negotiations with literary tradition confidently, and in a voice already decisive and original. In several poems, Wyley recalls with admiration her father's meticulous and intimate investment in the books he loved. Their printed words, the literary canon, the presence of a "full book shelf / arranged in library order", and his readerly example, offered her inspiration, security and the "smell of comfort / and wonder", she acknowledges. But in 'Books' she emphasises that his careful reverence is not a mode she can fully follow. Her own books are, by contrast, often "battered" or "creased" from being part of everyday life — "marked with breakfast coffee spilt / on the earliest 50A ride to work", or containing "breadcrumbs long left over / suddenly flaking free from words". The conceit voices her belief that writing, and especially poetry, must escape the preserve of the book-lined room, must be enjoyed in the traffic of ordinary life, and must derive from and be marked by it, to be fully alive and sustaining. For poetry to sing, it must first express and respond to the actual and to ordinary things — an "unemptied bathroom cup / not yet scrubbed of toothpaste stains", "the heather-headed lanes of Howth", "endives, guacamole, fettucine". Imaginative transubstantiation — evoked so provocatively in the volume's title — must begin in the bread of daily life.

Wyley's award-winning second collection — *Socrates in the Garden* (1998) — foregrounds these core aims, and her wish to situate seriousness of thought and artistry within the quotidian and the natural. She has spoken of her regard for Yeats's practice of composing prose statements of a poem's "subject" before he embarked on actually writing, and also of her sense that an emerging poem is usually its own best critic or advocate, forcing the writer to simplify, clarify or intensify as needed. The collection strongly reflects those commitments in its unobtrusive formal precision and its accessibility of language. Characteristically in these poems, long sense-units that capture complex sequences of feeling and juxtapositions of perspective are carefully modulated in stanzas composed of deceptively simple short run-on lines with an underlying ease of syntactical flow. The effect is to accentuate the force and movement of single lines, and to heighten our attention to the texture and sound of these short clusters — there are rarely more than four or five words per line — thereby emphasising what William Carlos Williams called the "dynamization" of the emotions or insights that each line can embody or produce. Another hallmark of the poems is a repeated movement between thoughts of the past and a focus on the actuality of the present, in ways which stress how the remembered inflects our experience of the ordinary and the actual, but is in turn itself inevitably reshaped by that later experience. In 'Hair', for instance, a woman thinking of her beloved is jolted into fresh understanding and new emotion by finding a pile of his scissored hair, which draws her thoughts of him, and herself, into surprised new combinations. 'Sean Nós Singer' acknowledges that while life can only be lived "in this world", the "undergrowth past" (whether actually shared with another or conceived in imagination) is a constant presence "pulling us back together"— a richly ambiguous phrase which both attests to and celebrates the power of words to not only evoke life but bring us into it more closely or attentively.

In *Poems for Breakfast* (2004), as that title announced, the aspirations of the previous volume, and of earlier poems like 'Books', for a writing that might be both about and part of the daily world, and nourish us as directly as possible, become even more marked. This collection is overwhelmingly centred in the immediate. Images of writing, and references to books, music and painting abound, but almost always as initiating moments encouraging an eager return to the movement and energy and savour of daily life and human exchange. The title poem and many others assert that Art is most valuable when it serves to make us see more clearly, returns the world to us in heightened and intensified forms, and offers us a "door forever opening." In 'Painter at Work', for instance, a picture "fills a space, then is with you everywhere"— is "over the kitchen work-top where you scoop /muesli" but also "pinned high in the sky over streets you walk down". To stroll through Dublin with an architect friend is "to see things differently" and to notice for the first time richness and possibility that has "always been there" awaiting discovery. In

"Somebody has died close by" bereavement flowers and notes in "a lane that I trudge up / every day and evening,/ not noticing much" unexpectedly transform the perception of that place, loosening a rich freight of thoughts and feelings "from the cupped hands of that moment".

In *To Wake to This* (2009) such moments of heightened attention are a repeated source of wonder and appreciation. Whether figured as an actual physical waking from sleep, a shifting into alert perception of reality after being immersed in a book or music or memories, or being jolted into new ideas and feelings by what is encountered or seen in the ordinary course of life, the "waking" of this collection's title is explored and craved in its poems as a sustaining revelation, and continual source of discovery. Throughout, one is conscious of Wyley's joy in the pleasures of family, motherhood, friendships, and the richness of everyday possibilities; and conscious, too, of her pleasure in and commitment to the task of trying to express that joy, and the wonder of "waking," in her poetry. 'Little Heart', 'Magpie' and 'First Words', for instance, enviously and admiringly observe her young daughter's emergence into language and teeming imagination, as what is seen and heard, part-comprehended and acutely apprehended, swirl into new combinations in the child's mind, and are eagerly absorbed and enjoyed. For the child, everything is fresh, and newly-acquired words are almost literally able to bring things to life — with the utterance of "meow" a "story cat / leaps from her mouth". The distinction between the printed words of a book she reads, and the life and sounds around her, seems momentarily erased, too, as her "breakfast jam / smudges on the page". This is the condition of perception and experience the poems in the collection themselves aspire to, although Wyley knows well that it can only be simulated or briefly conjured into being in words, and that the writer's and artist's task is always to some extent a vain effort at recovery: "our pencils and brushes scraping for life". In 'Notebook Shop' poems are imagined being prevented from being written down when "a wind blows the door open" and allows them to flow free rather than be "trapped" in a book. In 'Lucky' a man absorbed in thoughts of Monteverdi's music is fortunate when "startled" back into seeing the complexity and beauty of the world around him. And 'The Page Within' — a pivotal poem in Wyley's work to date — charges that the poet should write, above all, "for the page within": using words as a means for writer and reader alike to move more deeply into the uncertainty of the self, as well as a means to more fully attend to and appreciate the "treasure" of the potentially talismanic everyday things around us. Some of the finest poems in this collection are amongst the most minimalist in their style — in 'Little Heart', 'Bird', 'To Wake to This', 'Lucky' and others, lines are stripped down to just one or two words, inviting us to pressure and relish their particularity and suggestiveness, and to linger with them even as we are conscious that they also impel us forward as they become part of a larger "chain" of connections and perceptions. In this work, language itself is intimately part of the treasure available to be unfreighted and enjoyed.

Such artful shaping characteristically distinguishes the first of Wyley's new poems collected here — 'Borrowed Space', the source of this volume's title. Its tightly controlled tercets and precise movements between moments of dense attention and verbal concentration are reminiscent of elements of Emily Dickinson's technique. And that echo is both deliberate and appropriate. The "borrowed" space of the title — in the simplest sense, just a house loaned by friends — is also, by implication, the space of writing itself, in which all words and ways of using them are marked to some extent by the way they have been used in the past by earlier writers; and the space of reading, too, which temporarily stills the "clamour" of daily life as we turn inward to its invitation to a restorative sense of order and fullness. But in these new poems Wyley's allusions to the river of tradition are easily collegial, often very witty, never studied or showy, and always fertile. The challenge of trying to make the moment stay in words, of knowing the self or the world better, of telling "of ordinary things intimately" is, they remind us, the familiar task poets have always faced; and to take up that challenge afresh is inevitably to strive both to extend and honour what has been done well before. In 'Julius Caesar had a Pet Giraffe', for instance, Wyley playfully echoes Yeats's rag-and-bone shop of old materials needing renewal as she surveys her own "debris of work — apple butts / to bin, bitten pencils, new words to sharpen". Yeats's fantastic bestiary of poetic devices, and anxious meditation on the quest for new images and inspirations, is reconceived and modified here in contemporary terms, with the "tap-tap of things beginning" on a laptop giving way to thoughts first of "a giraffe printing curious across the page" in a child's book, and then — in imaginings that are both fabulous and ominous — of that print-bound giraffe being "savaged by lions in Caesar's arena". The poem desires "what might come alive" from books, but is also acutely conscious that the space of reading and also of writing — alas — inevitably requires at least a temporary turning away from the ordinary it both feeds on and ultimately aims to feed. To write is figured in this collection as both an "expectant dark" — pregnant with possibility — and as an "unforgiving dark" of struggle and frequent failure, and separation from life. In her early poem 'Orpheus' Wyley imagined the Greek musician and poet reflecting on his inexorable need to sing, and his recognition that, despite the intensity of his love for Eurydice, "there would be no music if you were beside me". In these new poems, the hopes and insights voiced in early poems such as this, and in 'Books', repercuss in more awkward, complex forms, often turning on the paradoxical recognition that loss is not only inevitable but necessary to poetry, and that writing can only produce a momentary stay, a gem-like moment of vision, amidst the perpetual flight of impressions and experiences.

Yet the signature of these new poems is their eager attention to experience and to the problematic task of honouring and representing it in words. In 'Rue Soufflot' and 'Unbearable' the singularity of what can be seen and felt fuel expectant excitement and a yearning to record things as fully as possible. In the closing poem, 'The News From Here' internet articles and a book are put aside in favour of attending to the more "urgent mark" of a child, and the wonder of a seashore where there are "winkles to pluck, / bladderwrack balls to burst". At the end of this beach day its yield is written in words on the sand — words hence to be soon swept away by the tide, like the lover's name in Spenser's sonnet. But those fragile words are simply and fundamentally affirmative: "We Are Here".

Readers who have not encountered Enda Wyley's work before will find in this volume a core selection of her poetry, which charts the impressive course of her achievements over more than twenty years. Readers who already know her writing well will find in the new poems published here much to admire, the assurance that her voice and style are continuing to evolve, and the enviable promise of what we can anticipate next.

— James L. Pethica
Professor of Irish Studies and Modern Drama,
Williams College, USA
Former Director of the Yeats International Summer School

from **Eating Baby Jesus** (1993)

"I shouted hoarsely, 'It was just a joke.
You mustn't leave me, I'd rather be dead.'
He smiled calmly, terribly, then he spoke;
'Don't stand out here in the rain, he said.'"
— Anna Akhmatova, 1911

Wedding Gift

In Memory Raymond Carver, 1938-1988

Salmon, leaping eternally against a well-lit sky,
bend ecstatic towards the waterfall, in the wedding gift you painted.
Like Chekhov, I map new routes from the town where I'll soon die

but now and then I stop, admiring these fish that try
to tussle free from the river; a push, then they've succeeded —
salmon leaping eternally, against a well-lit sky.

If I'd even a year! I make a list; eggs, hot chocolate, buy
cigarettes labelled 'Now', at last book that Antarctica ticket!
Like Chekhov, I map new routes from the town where I'll soon die

and must continue the struggle upstream, despite the lie
I lived; once drunk, wife-leaver, bum – but now, like determined
salmon leaping eternally against a well-lit sky

in this picture you gave us for our last fling; that high,
sad, tacky affair in a Reno Chapel, after the blood I'd coughed.
Like Chekhov, I map new routes from the town where I'll soon die

and am travelling faster now, suddenly floating high
where my poems make me beloved; yet still I watch over my head
salmon leaping eternally against a well-lit sky —
like Chekhov, I map new routes from the town where I'll soon die.

The Obstacle

after Cavafy

You have arrived before you are home,
before even a door is opened,
before a hand could rise high,
or sweet meals colour a hungry end —
you are with me, dusting silence
into plastic refuse sacks,
you walk shadows across my sunlit carpet lines
and by my desk have thumbed my chin up
to face your *yes* or *no*.

But there is no place for you here,
where trees whisper an activity
less assuming, more real than yours,
and days are the delicate stir
of private questions in this room's pots.
In my head, though absent, you arrive
and I am shocked by a definite barrier.
How could there be hope for you here?
Through my shutters I peep content.
When you depart, silence is the dancer,
beautiful, justified at my front door.

Orpheus Speaks

Even in the catacombs I will be singing,
though my head has been severed, then hurled down the Hebrus
by those frenzied women, I will be heard still calling
your name, across the snows of Northern Tancus

or deep in freezing caverns. No wedding tune can move me.
I have made my own song, cried for you beside the Strymon river,
yet knew there would be no music if you were beside me.
I could not have intrigued stones, oak trees, the curious tiger

if hell's three-headed dog had never growled
or Ixion tied to a cruel, burning wheel had ceased
to spin. If the ferryman had brought me back across the fen

that lay between us, you would not hear me now roam
the black world of our separation, still singing in this tomb.
So, against warning I will turn, to lose you again and again.

Poems Whispered in Leningrad, 1940

in memory Anna Akhmatova

May I never, as she did, on scraps of paper
have to pass my rhyme on — like a mantle of ermine
she shared in the cold, a loved verse safer
burnt, a memorised fire in the minds of women
who queued outside Leningrad jail in prayer
and whispered her blue-lipped lines for their men
taken by the guards to God knows where.

May I never have to walk the empty streets,
dependant as she was on that hard-made song
surviving by being repeated, softly repeated —
never be afraid I'll lose a word, get the poem wrong,
or fear in the early hours that I might be arrested
and in airless prison trains with roofs of iron,
exiled — all my books, my pens confiscated.

And yet, I must make the harsh journey, I know,
from Kazan through to Tashkent station —
seeing from my own heart's Siberian window,
just as she did, those people's devastation.
How else can my words become the cooling
noise of water, a tree's shade in tortuous heat —
how else can they become flowers blooming
in a besieged and starving street?

Mandelstam

Hurting,
you pushed skyward

your own dream
high and fearless

above skeleton traps
the steel man dug

for the flying few.
Perfectly,

you made all your own.
Yes, even Petrarch

is you, Osip —
Italian purity translated

deep in Petersburg snow.

Home from Sydney

1.

On the Lloydiana we should have sailed
with those eight packages rolled
between futon slats and feathers.

I would have liked slow days
to thumb my market books
from Sydney through to Tilbury terminal —

liked to cruise long hours with you,
unroll from travel newsprint perhaps,
our favourite, sculpted Freemantle head

or play cricket with Drysdale's boys, painted
thin and young, out in the gold-town sticks,
now preserved in our picture-frame.

On the Lloydiana we should have sailed
with our beloved things – not separated from them
with a foolish half-year wave.

2.

Some cold December day they'll come,
a sudden doorstep surprise,
unexpected as the bulging backache silence

we pushed despairingly between us
on that empty parquet floor
when the Lloydiana left.

How can we share things now?
The Melbourne yabby pump we bought,
those felt-clothed antique dolls —

will they be most sore observers
of our faded hearts? Or will the travelled boxes
open fresh smells in the Dublin hall —

Blue Mountain air and Bondi surf
spilling out
to stun, unite us with the past.

Eating Baby Jesus

On a Monday mitch, for something to do,
Gummo crunched Alpen with eucharist —
a ten year old's breakfast
of roughage and baby Jesus
creamed in a stolen chalice.

No stained glass here,
no well-kept shrine —
a graffitied church
on a housing estate.
On the priest's roof-top,

housekeeper screeching
in Gummo's head
like last night's lifted cars,
he is a young protester —
a prisoner raining down

piss on the prison yard.
He can climb the school railing later —
tall, iron tree with rusted spikes
and there, lodged in its roots
on the playground side,

a brick.
He wants to send concrete ripples
through the window sea
of classroom heads bobbing on calm.
A child's face splinters within

and crayon blood figures out
sudden red on a sum copy page.
For this I could dangle Gummo,
roping him upside down
like the kittens they gut live

on this wasteland's torture branch;
but I know he is fast away,
his hair damp as council walls,
his pulse racing a ghetto beat.
He will run through row upon row

of boxed grey —
hope always dim for him
as headlights in winter smog
from the coal-burning tombs of babies
named after soap stars

and a visiting pope.

Where Poems Begin

It was always your suggestion,
simple as the twenty pence challenge
placed on our holiday chalet mantelpiece —
an idea
that shook from our heads
like magic seaside dust,
Tory Island's one-eyed
monster, upside down
lands, children's mysteries,
all sprinkled stories
in evening copy book lines
and all mouthed
from sunburnt faces
when you returned to read.

Often I have lost these lines,
on purpose sometimes,
but know that when
your smile suggests,
I will go to where they are,
kept safe between pages
in some crowded
drawer perhaps,
waiting again
and again to be found,
to add memory
and words
to a memory —
my father moving always
in a room lined with books.

Books

My father always kept his books clean.
When reading, he balanced those precious words
on his table of well-ironed corduroy thighs
and advised that, like him, I be careful to touch
with two fingers (briefly)
only the corners of each finished page
when ready to move on —
though often I would watch his hand
slowly feel across the turning thoughts,
like a man's light touch in reluctant farewell
to a face he has come to love.

Mine were the new but battered ones,
covers bent far back, edges creased.
'It's beyond me how you can manage
to mangle every one,' he'd taunt,
but I was finding in each mauled book
a home for my own ways; I liked sand
shifting where the pages joined in story,
breadcrumbs long left over
suddenly flaking free from words,
and split hairs forked above lines
as a diviner's stock over water —
all meant more than any signature to me
that these books were mine.

Mine, marked with breakfast coffee spilt
on the earliest 50A ride to work,
the back-seat windows
my jolting, smogged-up pillows
while words unstuck the sleep in my eyes.

He sat with his books in our sitting room —
one finger pressed each line to life
while his tongue between his teeth
wet his upper lip.

Closed, he marked those books
with old greeting cards
or writings from St John
he'd discovered that February
in his fortieth year.
He never drank or smoked again
but he still took Marx down
from his full book-shelf
arranged in library order.
He was ever suspicious and knew
which ones had just gone missing,
borrowed when I hoped he wasn't looking.

Just when he had no need to worry,
he chose my leaving home
to hide the books
behind his wardrobe door — the titles
like his absent daughter's name
he could never say again
without remembering.
Father, we will meet surprised, someday,
both reaching for the same line.

Measuring

1. DEATH AMONG ORDINARY THINGS

In the morning we found him,
skeins of light knotted
through his still antennae —
unmoving nightflier combs.

It was too late to pull him
from our unemptied bathroom cup
not yet scrubbed of toothpaste stains.
His stout body drowned

he floated in our sink above the tiled floor —
a moth, dead in the small ceramic pool
beside the shaving blades and vitamins,
such ordinary things.

And so, I see you too, trapped
in a frowsty space of usual things —
bird-stained windows darkening nearby,
a bedroom window gradually closing.

Who can rescue you now from your final hours,
weak as the consommé they spoon you?
Your closing minutes a predictable effete pulse
the hospice aide is pressing.

There will be no more difficult stairs
for concerned arms to help you up,
no oversized clothes for you to button,
no carefully chosen diet easing your digestion.

While we fade from you, as we will one day
from each other, Jesus framed
points to his bleeding heart
lit sacred above your limbs.

In this room of prayer and anticipation
you are weakening fast and seem to me,
beneath your last day's clammy sheets,
like distressed wings, netted.

2. Sweet Pea and the Greyhound

'He'll beat you from here to Dublin,'
the Leitrim farmer bargained,
'and you in a car, he's that fast.'
So, she let him buy his want —
slender blue-grey Rossinver pup,
because she knew that soon
he could never exercise hope again,
be able even to walk up field
the distance marked for his training hound.

Back home, she watches him — her man,
swinging with less strength each day
on their garden's faded canopy chair —
hears his breathing slow down, crack
like the kennel door now scratched apart
by the newly bought, neglected dog.
They've warned he may give in,
and, afraid of what to say if asked,
she is distracted, chases in the wind
string the postman left behind,
hoping to tame with twine

her sweet pea before it grows wild —
but already its petals
flapping like wings,
its white and frantic flowers,
have arrived high up
where it is not yet
her time to follow.

3. MEASURING

After, everyone's gulping whiskey,
glad of the loud demands
their empty glasses can slam down.
More quick undiluted shots
and, shaking death off,
they find a silent comfort
in each others' reeking closeness.

But I am suddenly thinking how,
just an hour ago, we marked
our measurements on the kitchen wall —
arguing that shoes be discarded,
tippy-toes not allowed,
that raised hair be flattened,
or sloped shoulders straightened.

A too thick nib, an unsteady hand
can make all the difference, we knew,
and challenging each other's conclusions,
voices raised momentarily,
we forgot that overhead he was ill —
was measuring different things,

how long it took him
to touch his face to hers and whisper
words of love he'd never told her
in all their forty years together;
then choked with regret,
terrified by his lack of time,
his calculations became hysteria

like the bedside bell she rang in panic,
making us rush upstairs, the kitchen left empty,
all our tape and pens discarded.
Now they assure her it's usual practice
to take him away so soon like this
for the final preparations,

and hearing them ease his weight downstairs
she knows he is going out
for the last time —
only his memory left
marked by us on love's wall.

Cúil Aodha Singer

for Iarla

You are different
when you sing the aching notes
your fathers praised
beneath thatched roofs,
whistled in shebeens,
or rippled for lovers on the shore
when wind rushed fear
into the boats of the fish hunter.

I had heard of you
and your difference
that called old men
to your southern place,
where sean-nós moves
strong and natural
as the strange eastern ship
your father built in the haggard.

But only when by accident
I find this room in a city bar
crowded with the listening silence
your voice evokes,
can I forget your tiny stature,
your loneliness, the arguments
we hated but had, and wonder
instead at the power of you

when you steady yourself
with a chair back,
touch eyelashes

against your cheek bones,
tilt your face high,
and shake rafters
with your song.

After, the clap of approval
and gasp of praise.
Maith thú, go h-álainn, ó thuaidh...
and the question always,
Cad as duit?

Where you come from
can only be found
in the secrets of your song
we are lucky to hear.
A rún, a rún,
won't you come back soon,
to the love that is always burning.

Venus de Milo

About Monet we fought
at the Place de La Concorde.
Where exactly had he shaped rooms for lilies?
And our words wedged between us —
uncomfortable as stones
from the Tuilleries in our shoes.
Angry, you said my bottom
was large and round as those women's
under trees in the October rain,
so that before the pyramid gallery
I wished we had never held
over our heads in the thin city gardens
this broken umbrella dispute.

In the Louvre I wished I was
without arms, without legs —
the Venus de Milo —
useless, beautiful treasure,
but receiver of all your smiles.

The Waitress has Transformed

The waitress has transformed.
Her flat hair curls,

her pale lips redden.
She has seen your face

and transformed.
As I hide my face in your chest

I am jealous that you
continue to order more —

endives, guacamole, fettucine —
until in the sea of food I sink

to watch you place
a gherkin in her mouth.

Wedding Bed

You will make noise
and more growing chatter
on this bulk of cotton and hard foam
we squeeze stairward.
It knows it will be loved
and is difficult in its importance —

refusing to push easily past corners and ledges.
So we catch it by its angled ends
and heighten it with reddening effort
over the freshly painted bannister
and under your low shade,
cursing its monster size.

You and your man may stub your nails
against the edges of this bed,
may hurt your backs to dress it,
drop food crumbs, itchy on its belly,
lose loved house things forever
in the dust and dark beneath its springs.

But always we'll curl up happy in it,
always together here, you boast.
It's dangerous to compare, I say,
but still you taunt me
with his name and the sadness
that split me from him.

You shake my memories like feathers
from your gaping pillow-case
leaving me twisting remembrance

on your floral mattress, this bed's first hurt.
I hear the heavy silence tease like wedding bells
and tighten my fists against the past.

Love Goes Home

for Gitte

Love, in this early hour of our final day,
parting seems easy to you
as the pressing into my hand
of a list of things you have left me to do,
when you're gone away.

> I will try to emulate you;
> try to dust our past clean
> like dirt webs swiftly wiped
> from your thread-leafed spider plant
> or the dark-covered books you give me,
> too heavy, you say, to pack —
> will try when your name
> falls through my door
> on your still incoming mail
> to newly address, then forward on
> all my thoughts of you.

But love, in the early hours of our last day,
do not ask me to call goodbye,
or wave at your bobbing back-window head.
I know the taxi that takes you away
will fume a black image in the morning sky —

you nestling somewhere else
into a waiting bed, finding the home you left
for a while, in her warm stirring pulse.

Municipal Gallery Favourite

after Patrick Scott

I want to blow again
down the fine straw
of my childhood days
that sunburst —
huge orange gasp
splattered on the canvas.

It was our favourite painting,
magic as penny wishes
below the winged Children of Lir
in the Garden of Remembrance,
necessary as stale bread in paper bags
for the ducks in Herbert Park
beautiful as the kite-high view
of Killiney Bay
we clambered after up Victoria Hill.

Too bored by dull attendants,
pompous guides or parents,
we spun many races each week,
dared one another to whizz shouting down
the great bannister slide
and leap again up the marble stairs;

then loved to burst
with our bare feet
tar bubbles on the summer roads,
loved tree swings
over secret backyard jungles,
the ivy huts we hid in,

woven across orchard walls — but more,
this orange, paint-blown shape
that made our church clothes casual,
our thoughts simple, arrogant
on Sunday visits;
'Bet we could do that too,
if we'd paper big enough!'

Now I stroll the gallery with you
during holy hours.
A man is talking about a painting.
I stop and join the intent group.
Afterwards, I find
a cushioned bench to rest on.

Somewhere below
I know the sunburst favourite
is dulled by basement dust
and lack of funds;
I try to catch its light again
in another piece nearby —

a grey figure stumbles
along a white strand curve,
while behind mountains
only tips of gold
suggest a fallen warmth.

Swimmer

Nobody liked the rain.
huddled under their deck-chair shelters
the drenched people wondered
at how she swam alone
against the waves like that,
her long arms arching *hello* to the drops
that only widened even more,
the sunless ocean grey.

Then for a moment in the fattening wet,
these people saw the illusive madness
they had believed in when small.
She swims, they thought,
but does not move;
only the slanted ripples twirl,
twisting her strokes
as once their toy spinning top
had spun their simple world around.

They imagine perfection —
her hair spiked straight beneath the blue,
her limbs curved ivory soft,
her toes dipping whirlpools through the sea —
but when she rises, they meet with dying eyes,
see the ageing yellow flesh, her stomach sag
as if the water had laid seed there,
and remembering that the earth was never flat,
that the swimmer moves always with the tide,
they watch the rain fall on.

Fall

for Niamh Hyland

When sea rolled day into the skyline,
you were there, riding on a horse
across Bundoran sands, welcoming me.

I remember the looseness of stirrup,
the slide of reins against thumb
and my novice trot on the sand.

You followed
and only saw what I felt —
a sudden speed that left you far behind.

I could not turn,
felt my body creak with saddle crutch,
saw the jump of shore and wave ahead,

wondered would I reach their line
but with each quickening hoof knew
my body was about to slant

free from that too wild race.
This fall has sent you running above me,
figures gaping over the cliff edge.

Others send ropes down.
Panic has crashed like boulder clouds
against the sea-birds' flight.

But I could lie here silent,
watchful forever of this horse.
He moves to lick the ocean cream

and I slip through my fingers
the beach's damp, before being hit
by the world's mad rush for me.

Triangle Path

for Eugene O'Rourke

That Whit weekend, with an early start,
he cut a thick triangle path
through the tall grasses of our sleep,
heaving his sixty years
across buttercup and ragwort,
to sting cool
his hand blisters
at the river stones.

Loud as the water moves,
stronger than sun pebbles
glinting on our morning bed,
he blinked our curtains wide,
pushed our eyes attentive
to his style —
now wood chipped shapely,
guarding its green domain.

When he entered,
his smell was more filling
than our dry bread and tea —
his words, fresh flower juice
wetting that day awake.
He shook his work like garden pieces
from two boots and said,
'That ash was tough.'

But we with our brief city freedom
have no time — managing half-nods
behind our holiday books and newspaper.

Out he went again.
We were relieved —
not knowing that when we fell,
a still branch beneath hospital linen,
that we would struggle too, like him,
to walk the triangle path
and carve our lives in the ash logs.

A Life

You have made a list
of happenings and lines
and will never revise it,
you say,
preferring instead
to repeat what's safe
when the social moment asks.
You have made a list
of stories and jokes
of men and places
and say it is your life.

I mark a circle
on your Guinness head
with this Cointreau dip —
small, curved glass, liqueur-filled,
it plunges deep into stout,
emerging upright to be plucked
later from your half-gone pint later.
Over and over you down
this bold mix of Irish cream
and your words expand.

We are children pushing
through books
on a grown-up's shelf,
finding a golden goose —
and now you, beside me,
erasing your list, begin:
'I was born when daffodils grow.'

from **Socrates in the Garden** (1998)

i.m. John Forbes, poet.
Died Melbourne January 23rd, 1998, aged 47

> *"Somewhere in the heaven*
> *of lost futures*
> *the lives we might have lived*
> *have found their own fulfillment."*

— Derek Mahon, 'Leaves.'

Mother

There is a room in my head, to which you often come,
orchid gifts wet with rain in one hand,
in the other your love
wrapped in a cut-out newspaper piece
you've saved just for me
or maybe sealed tight in irregular pots
of home-made jam.

You come in and we quickly leave behind
the thorny rose-gardens of our grown-up fights.
I smooth out the creases in your gentle face
I know I've often caused —
while you, keeping me from the shabby coldness
of this outside world,
put the last stitch on my coat.

Journey

You give me T-shirts
fresh with your smell,
trousers that flap love
against my ankles, cool
as your assurance with life.
You tie red ribbons
to the handles of my bag —
silk reminders of what's mine.

For must not every journey have
the pusher and the pushed?
When the ambulance men
bumped you out of our house
that late August day
you tried to clamber back
up that stairs again.
Don't let me go, you cried.
We folded night-shirts,
packed toothpaste, underwear,
blocked our ears against the voice
we were not sure
we would ever hear again.

Then mother, your mother came
speaking in lilting Clonakilty tones:
Don't worry girl, I'd never leave you;
her voice a song dragging you
from a hospital room
far away to where
she'd arrived from life
long before you.

Even Indians, their brown faces
white-teethed in your near-death dream,
dragged their boats onto a beach
they'd sanded on your sheets
and tried to bring you with them,
tempting you across a river away
from your children's toys and summer things.

We could not push you
where you would not go
not wanting you to go ourselves.

In the shadow of next door's wild rhubarb
mad nettles and vicious dog,
the figure-of-eight rose bed
you once dug has gone —
where you knelt,
trowel in your gloved hand
your face smiling under
a bright headscarf,
to see us leap home,
free from school at last
squealing delights,
climbing the old holly tree
or hiding our secrets
in the old compliant oak —
our uncouth tree-house
hanging there over
Bourke's mansion, his orchard,
his horses and fast cars.

But you are still here
in this garden
under the cherry tree —

your words its blossoms
against my face
Out there, it'll all work out.
Don't worry, child, go now.
You press the bag into my hand
and your fingers, warm
in the small of my back, push.

Socrates in the Garden

for Peter Sirr

In his world he moves,
January light fooling
this place into beauty —
broken glass glittering
on the flat's side lane,
white graffiti translucent
on the school wall;
Pushers out! Egg Head.
Fuck off. Wanker Meehan.
Old shoes, their laces tied,
dangle over electricity wires,
beside pulled-apart phones
flung there, high above
burnt mattresses, gutted cars
and rusting bikes,
used needles jabbing the way
the children go to school.

Parents yell,
their calls like cigarette ash
billowing out
in front of their washing
hung from shabby balconies,
the grandmothers busy below
with Moore Street prams piled
with fruit, football hats, lighters,
fireworks and wrapping paper —
all the stolen seasons trundling
their way to the market
down roads Matt Talbot roamed

with drink, then manic prayer,
his chains the size of a horse's trace
wrapped round his body
one hot June day
where he fell on Granby Lane.

And in this world,
Margaret goes to get married
in a horse-drawn carriage
around Stephen's Green.
All skin and bone,
pneumonia choking
her final days,
her name will become a ribbon
and light on the Christmas tree,
an embroidered square
on a patch-work quilt
hung in a vast, cold place
where the young priest talks only to women,
the wind outside blowing litter —
caged pigeons set free from rooftops,
rising up oblivious as gulls from the Liffey.

In his world he moves,
his head slanted against doorways,
his cheeks bruised
with the cut of a city night.
Hearing the cathedral chime
hourly, cheeky, melodic.
Three Blind Mice ...
In Dublin's Fair City ...
He queues at the soup kitchen's door
choosing food
over the bell ringer's charm.

His hunger, slouching
in second-hand clothes
against the city wall,
is so acute it sends
early morning nightmares —

how the stained glass
in Nicholas of Myra cracks,
how major Sirr rises from his grave
pulling St Werburgh's apart,
strutting down Thomas Street to watch
Emmet's delerium beheaded!

And sometimes into his world
you move,
cooling his fever,
wetting his mouth
with fresh basil leaves
of hope, lifting his thoughts,
so that far away
over the copper domes,
the shut-up, run-down flats,
he can see in the garden
Socrates —

his toes cracked, his robe
thrown across shoulders
chipped with neglect,
part of his nose fallen lost
among polite glass-houses,
herbaceous borders
and Victorian signs.
But his stare is deep-eyed,
and his thoughts are river sounds,

original like rain
on this bright day.
He is finding a space for you both
in the otherwise wild
of your mid-lives, letting
your hard city fall away
with each push of the gate
inwards to this green heaven.

Run to his shape,
the willow trees whisper,
Pull our leaves
like hair from his face —
find his eyes
staring, questioning you.

(Botanic Gardens, July 1997)

Litany for a Sunny Day

Cherry blossoms
under our bottoms
on the roll of the cricket field,
the girl with the bright face,
her knees hunched close
to a bicycle
splayed black
on the Trinity green,
you fingering the dimples
at the base of my back,
your new boots
not creased, not dirty,
yet painful on your toes,
the woman brushing, brushing
her blonde hair in Front Square,
the Italian nosing his kiss
into the mesmerised
student's cheeks,
the fair on the Green
with no books we like,
except one journal
of eighteenth century medical ads —
Samuel Steel, tooth surgeon
on Ormond Quay, makes
artificial teeth so neat
they may be worn several years
without being taken out
of the mouth. Dr Lowther's
powders and drops
operate insensibly
and may be taken by the fair sex

at all times with the greatest safety ....
Much later, you walk me home
and I ask *Do you love me?*
not caring for words in reply,
just your lips flaring red
as the park tulips — the moon
an ivory eye, spying at us
from the old city wall.

Magpie

for Ger O'Shea

Outside my door today
a magpie
dead under the garden trellis
beneath the shadow
of the bathroom window.

And so glass-eyed,
one-winged, half-eaten,
so dusty, unmoving,
that I could only
bring him into my home —

place him
on the clash of carpets
with old rugs,
where his loneliness
became mine.

Pirandello plays
bent with much reading,
Callas soaring
out over
Fitzwilliam Square,

empty grate
that will not house fire,
like the tube empty
of whiskey
on my desk.

City outside,
fresh with sounds
I will not partake in,
let me watch this bird
loose his soul,

to confer with you
my beloved things —
beneath a ceiling
that crumbles
and will someday fall.

Ghosts

for Jack Gilligan

The first, her shape lovely
on the chip-board shelf
at the end of my teenage bed,
Catcher in the Rye, The Bell Jar,
Sartre, Martin Luther King, Garp,
all lightly dusted by her feet,
swaying, gently swaying,
hippy necklace of the time
loosely falling like rosary beads
through her rhythmic hands —
night-time angel watching me.

Then sister, what of that spectre shape,
standing boldly before us, in the dark
cottage near Rossinver
a week before your wedding day,
waking you to my breath
heaving in disbelief, just as before
on grandad's sloping old mattress
when the heavy dreams hurt
and I was a child.
It's all right, go back to sleep.

And in Westport
in that windowless room,
three shepherds gaped
at my drowsy shape,
their hands helpless
at their mammoth sides,
their nails caked in the muck

of Slieve More, their tweed caps
faded by too much rough wind and sun.
On Achill, days later, I found
their names on a headstone
I clambered to,
over the deserted village wall.
Three men drowned at the foot
of this mountain and saved in vain
their sheep from the sea.
Then I felt again
their awful presence near my bed,
their anxious mouthing in request;
We did not have time
to say goodbye,
tell them to remember us.

There have been others —
the room forever cold
at the top of the stairs,
in the house that defied superstition,
built west over a fairy path,
my father with a sock fat with stones
to clout the feckers with,
should they ever appear,
or your grandfather banging doors
in the gate-lodge at Castlefreak
a year to the day since his died.

Now
in the cross-shaped garden
on the hill of the city,
where the rebels' vision has cut
a poem into the granite wall,
Lir's stone children fall.

We hear their little feet
patter through your rooms,
opening the tall, wooden shutters,
searching the wide windowsills,
probing the vast chimney spaces.

Then turning into swans again,
they chip ornate, fading cornices
with their startled, white wings
and call in mythic sadness
for their lost, ageing father-king.
More lonely than these bird cries,
the strange banging against the wall
I heard, when he left me a year ago —
but now, these creatures' feathers fall
like scented air upon our heads.

We hear in their grief, our own,
and feel for others unresolved in their pain —
like Narcissus Marsh
forever locked in his small cage of books,
forever heard shuffling from shelf to shelf,
leafing through pages of loss,
desperate to find
his niece's written request
for a forgiveness he never gave her.
But the letter is never found.

(National Ballroom, Parnell Square, 1998)

Love Bruise

Afterwards she found it by accident,
shaped like a huge cougar prowling below
the jungle basin of her pelvic bone —
a tawny bruise that rode
her outer thigh's skin folds.

> *— I banged into a table edge,*
> *a car door bit into my side,*
> *where a knee-high daughter pinched*
> *greedy for my attention, I bruised.*

Days later it is fading —
becomes only a flash of pebble,
now purple, thumb-print size
under the waterfall roll
of dirt and suds from her morning shower.

> *— I grazed myself on the trellis nails,*
> *rusty diamonds on the garden wall,*
> *was hit by snowballs pelted at me*
> *one school-closed January day.*

She tells herself all these things,
over and over — even in her sleep.
They are easier than the truth;
the pain of your pull within her —
then away from her when you go.

Eight Short Love Poems

1. GIFT
after Auden

Something stirred in your head
and you came alive for me
out of the pillows and red sheets.
Something stirred.
I know what it was;
I put it there
while you were sleeping.
'I can never be different,
love me.'

2. PAROS NIGHT

I saw you hang
in the neck of the sky —
half-bitten nail and white tear-drop —
worry moon and a sad star
lapping your love to me
across miles of waves
to this island bed
where I am alone.

3. LIVES

When I was thirty
and did not know you,
there was an apartment

bright with light
from tall windows
looking out on trees
and buildings in Milan.

You were not there,
you did not know
those sun-filled days
of mine — how I curled
into another's body
in the Piazza Duomo
of each day and night
and, that time gone,
how I would find you
when you least knew
what was to come.

4. ORANGES

I cannot look
at oranges
without thinking
of you —
your hand
cooling my skin
with the roll
and sweetness
of soft fruit,
Gigli trembling in the room.

5. LILIES

Closed greens,
tight like a fist,
open bell-shaped
and pale
in the heat of our fight —

the scent of her
on you,
more powerful
than their smell.

6. MUSE

I raise my head to find
your face in cathedrals,
your breath rising slow
as Guinness factory smoke
curling brown statues
on this still afternoon sky.

No more the sound of you,
through rooms after dark,
the rustle of papers you read,
the scratch of nails on skin,
a line of a song begun then stopped —
all proof that you are there.

No more our two hearts burning
like oils mixed pure
in the home that was ours.

Though lies like kisses
marked your neck,
still you are my muse.

I raise my head to find
your face in cathedrals —
my joy, my sorrow
in you.

7. POSSUM

How long we stood that night,
our heads craning up
the paperbark tree,
searching for possums
ring-tailed and bushed,
the Melbourne dark hushed.
You, young and clever
threw earth balls high
to cause a sudden scamper —

It was the rush of my heart
wide-eyed in the quiet black,
not wanting to leave you yet,
hoping we could stay forever
like this, our faces
smiling, waiting —
the casual bend
of your hand in one pocket,
the other reaching for me.

8. STANDING IN THE RIVER

If you stand with me
in the river again,
I know the green goddess
will come

rising up
with her moss-soft love
to embrace us both
as before.

Talking to the Bees

for Maighréad Leonard

The city far away, in this place
silence falls with the Angelus bells
and *císte cróin* baked the night before
is today rough-round, a solid cake crucifix-marked,
uncut, not yet topped with loganberry red
she preserved in the heat of mid-July
till this woman of the kitchen is ready
to raise her head from prayer
and we are all given the nod to eat.

But once in this place, the city far away,
when the baking of bread was her mother's domain
she ran free of the house down the slope
where neighbours' farm-sheds seemed to bark,
so full they were of tied-down dogs
that the old mountain ash ahead
became her bright rowan guard.

And always the river rush
under the roadway loudly
or sometimes throbbing, approaching
like an imminent rare car
turning the road to school.
Then, what secrets could she have known —
her child's belly spread over the mossy wall,
her tiny fingers threading
the Dubhglas River's flow?
Did she stare so long that she felt
the whole world move before her
or see in the dark water-stones
things that might come to her?

Her husband going out to tell the bees
Tá se faoi chré, our son is dead,
the old magic and sadness waxed
in honey-caves for the bread
she carries in her satchel
on the two-mile path to class —
not knowing these things yet,
her little face bright as a rosehip berry,
her morning thought a young river trout
leaping, escaping the set night-lines.

Sean-Nós Singer

Sweet love, where else shall I live
if not in this world with you?
In other places where you go —
your eyes closed tight,
your song within, an *aisling* —
strong woman filling you with the same dream,
you sang in Irish on a classroom chair
your first day at school
not yet able to speak English,
your teacher knowing you had the gift.

Let me scramble with you
in the undergrowth past
where civil war bullets, hidden years under moss,
became, unknown to the adults,
playthings after school,
a force thrown against beech and oak —
hot and exciting as the tune in your head.

Let me sit in the old house
deep in trees in Cúil-Aodha
where bees make honey
and O'Riada makes music —
you practising new notes with him,
the piano lid raised and hummed into,
all the old singers dying.

Or in your mother's house
let me be with you
your grand-aunt's songs still trembling
in the laugh of her invalid sister
in the bedroom overhead —

you, a little boy listening, remembering,
repeating well into your grown-up years.

And so, if not in this world, my love,
I will find a place elsewhere
where, safe in the hollow of your neck,
I'll hear the songs that are yours calling
and feel the place that you come from
pulling us back together —

two children standing under an arch of snow
newly fallen on the bent tree's branches,
the warmth from our tightly held hands
fast melting winter into spring,
dispersing all cold with a kiss.

Hair

for Iarla

Just when I thought I knew it all —
how your body turns to mine in sleep,
how fresh your thoughts are in the morning —
I found in the knee-cave of my desk
your hair against the skirting board,
a pile of mysterious scissored black
turning brown, red, blonde
in the cup of my hand,
the room gone silent.
It was as if I knew something
new about you now —
was there at your birth,
the stillness of your death,
saw you do something without me.

And what could I do
but push out the window
of this country home
built west on a fairy path
and let your hair free with my love,
wide-winged like the slender-necked heron
wading the dark for you,
guiding you through the black
that spreads over these bush-hills,
the cry of strange animals far off.

And what could I say
but that you are beautiful.
For though the ebon mud
is deep under your feet,

though the trees whisper
a frightening ocean of spirits,
you are beautiful to me,
finding your way
bravely again uphill
to the light of our house
where love's bird resting taps away
all futile fights with its long-pointed bill
and is certain that from the yard fence —
cut wood now silver with lichens and moss —
the surprise of a new sally tree will grow.

Places You Have Found Me

On Pembroke Road,
or Fitzwilliam Square, staring up
from high-windowed basements
to the busy, railinged roads —
bicycles in halls,
coin phones constantly ringing,
landlords spying
from their downstairs rooms.
Or in bedsits overlooking the sea,
you have found me,
where salt and wind blew out
over Seapoint's martello tower
and granite pier walks,
the stench of our tiny kitchen's fry.

Places I have found you
on Trafalgar Terrace,
or Belgrave Square,
with wooden floors for dancing
naked to the singing
of Pierre Bensusan —
raised old baths to wash
love's sticky juices away,
large makeshift desks
to write to each other on,
both of us hating
the listening move
of a flatmate next door.

What loyalty I have
to those places
belongs to you —
your warmth in the mornings,
and the cracked walls of our lives
filling with deep-throated joy,
like the waking sparrows
crooning in the chimney pot,
strewing the fireplace
with twigs of mountain ash and beech.

Remember how you pulled
the weight of wide doors open
for me at unexpected hours,
lay your finger straight
on my lips
in whispered warning
and smiling, led me to your attic place,
both of us wide-eyed, breathless on each step?
Remember how we often left
that southern house
and crossed the fields
your grandmother blessed
every first day of spring
to make our own home
in the bump of rock and green
under Carraig a' Radhairc?

Now there is only summer.
Though the light is clear
and parks are full,
dust falls
on the windows
of my days.

You have cut the talisman
close to my throat,
have ripped
the painting we loved —
woman bent blue
on a backing
of Matisse white —

and have left to go wild
as the island in the west
you drive to,
and me alone in the house,
the door still banging,
the gravel on the lane
twitching for the crunch
of your return:
O, tar ar ais chugam,
tar ar ais chugam,
caillim thú go mór.

Five Definitions of a Butterfly

after the end of the IRA ceasefire, February 9ᵗʰ 1996

1.
Sometimes your name
can mean a cluster of weeds —
wild flowers lance-shaped, a bright orange glow
in the run-down tangle of our minds.

2.
I know long ago it was thought that witches
became you — stealing away on your wings,
eggs and cheese, milk or cream,
the farmer's eyes buttered with sleep.

3.
Then again, when you choose to,
you can become slang —
a young woman showily dressed,
making a quiet room giddy, capricious.

4.
Or I have seen you as a salt-water fish —
butterfly named, silvery flat in the tropical swamps,
your enormous mouth popping
the first and last vowel of your realm. Africa.

5.
But that night, you were a red admiral
flapping so frantic against the fluorescent light
that your craziness magnified in our glass net,
made us free you out into the night air.

How could we have known you would be
the very last light we would see
before electricity in our mountain home failed,
or that panic would beat —

a bat trapped indoors, its ultrasonic cries
echoing our black fear —
while we are left fumbling
in deep corners of the impossible dark?

The Soul Kisses Goodbye

I am the soul
that leaves your body
but at the door comes back
to kiss you once —
then, lonely, comes back
again and again,
my grief, jagged petals falling
on the floor of your mouth
that was always mine.

Twice, three times,
I become,
where the devil of pain
tries to dig its claws,
an angel at rest
on your shoulders —
a definite breeze
cooling down the heat
of your people's loss.

They lift their heads
from the side
of your bed
gone suddenly cold
and feel me kissing
your body goodbye,
over and over —
you who harboured me
so well in life
with love.

Note: *An t-anam a phóg an corp* — the soul that kissed the body — an old Irish story where the soul, having left the body cannot resist turning back to kiss it farewell repeatedly, having been protected by it in life.

from **Poems for Breakfast** (2004)

for Peter Sirr

Dish of a Moon

for Martin Drury

'... But then it's the light / that makes you remember.'
— Yehuda Amichai, 'Forgetting Someone'

He gets up to pace the house late at night —
is an anxious adult shutting doors, winding the clock,
pulling out plugs, making the dripping tap stop:
but on the landing, he looks out to check the light,

neighbours' roof-tops, his trees, the weather.
Wind tugs at the moon that is a memory
wide and yellow and he is a tide of worry
dragged back again to what he will never forget — his mother

kneeling beside him, her eight-year-old child, mopping
his night-time sweats away with her sweet made-up tune.
Lady moon, Lady moon, she sings to the high dish of a moon —
nearly forty years on, he swears he can still hear her singing

and feel her arms tight around him, her finger
pointing down to two foxes who have found their way
into the garden through the wood of time. Their eyes looking up say
The moon is a light left on — its light there to make you remember.

Two Women in Kosovo

for Orla Guerin

'I'm going to jump,' her sister whispers,
holding out her hand.
And so they jump together — so naturally
they might be girls again
leaping at waves on their holidays, jumping
across rivers on their way to school,
pulling each other over the road
to grown-up things.

From the side of the truck
out onto the rolling dust and scrub they jump,
tea and bread they've just eaten with the others
a thump in their stomachs when they fall.
Holding hands tight, they jump —
two women in Kosovo leaving behind
their children, their mother, their husbands
gunned down by soldiers
in a roadside café minutes before
and now a mountain of grief
being driven to a mass grave
somewhere these sisters will never find.

One of them looks back,
feels her whole life piled ugly there,
feels it was beautiful once —
the pull of her man reaching for her
in the middle of the night,
the bitter pain she knew when her four-year-old
left her for his first day at school,
her own mother calling her back home
on a cold winter's night.

Luck determines where we are born,
passes us through life
unscathed by violence.
Luck is this brave woman now
defying the brutal guards,
rising alive
from her pretend death
and the horror of corpses,
the people she's loved —
a frightened survivor pulling
her frightened sister forward,
a sister whispering 'jump!'

Cutting Hair on New Year's Day

Gulls land on the crumbs of the river,
and last year's bicycle gift
is wrapped yellow
in the reflections of the city, its wheels stirring
with each mullet's lazy flip of the Liffey's tail.

Holly wreaths still hang from the hotel's door
and Ormond Quay's sash windows
wink their prickly red-berry eyes
at you and me speeding through the streets,
speeding into the new year

like Flash Kavanagh, beloved priest of St Audeon's,
named after his twenty-minute mass —
the congregation below in Adam and Eve's
staring up the old hill in envy,
freezing from praying too long.

I have cold fingers, you a cold head.
I've cut through your hair this morning
and having no newspaper only Christmas wrapping
have sat you down over silver Santas, gold stars,
faceless angels — and clueless, have snipped away.

What do you work at yourself?
Do you want a number one or number two?
Oh how you trusted me! Your hair,
defiant like feathers, passing through my fingers,
blew with us to places we'd always longed to go —

Macchu Pichu, Greenland, The Cooley Pass
and would not let go of us. Even now it clings to us
walking gloveless, hatless through the quiet streets
on New Year's Day, exhaling the old year —
the new one not recognising the clean-cut you.

On My Father's Birthday

I saw silvery ancient lichen
that grows where the air is pure,

deep tap roots of the marram grass
holding the sand-dunes up —

those grasses we painted as children,
stood in jam-jars on our windowsills —

a cargo boat crossing the bay,

a dead sea-gull
his legs frozen and green,

the dog whelk shell I blew sand from
and later balanced on the bath edge,

the fluorescent pink dome of the Italian circus tent
far across in Booterstown, its lions roaring like sea,

sky-larks singing spring in,

sand under our nails and grating
the backs of our throats like arguments,

brent geese on mud-flats feeding on eel-grass
far from a Greenland peninsula,

bladderwrack sticking to stone
with a glue scientists crave,

ringed plovers and sanderlings,

oyster catchers with their twitting sounds
more high-pitched than the nervous gulls,

car windows glinting on James Larkin Memorial Road,
his hands a constant memory raised up over O'Connell Street,

terns flying away from Kilbarrack flats
and a top-shell shaped like an emperor's hat,

St Mary Star of the Sea, a holy stilt walker,

on the beach the red-coated father carrying one child
on his shoulder, laughing at the others racing the tide,

behind them a Sunday car sinking in the sand,
moss crawling up Mary's hundred-feet-high stone legs.

And they are us and you long before this day,
calling the sea a name we'd never heard before —

Thalassa, Thalassa, Thalassa,

and we chase after the *sliotar*
your hurley gives to those holiday waves,

we are young pups walking home with you over rabbits
sleeping deep in the sandy dunes of Cruit Island,

we are waiting for fresh fish got
from the currachs at Carrickfinn,

we are waiting for stories to come.

Marlborough Road

On Marlborough Road
the houses have names —
Aclare, Larnaca, Ardeevin,
Shalamar, Woodstock, Hazelhurst
and St Elmo on the way to the station
where the ghost creaked the gate long ago
one early winter morning
and became a wide-eyed Red Setter before me,
as frightened of a girl as I was of him,
our still worlds interrupted.

Going home up Marlborough Road,
I see the garden boats covered in canvas,
the spiked green railings
darker than the hedges
and the copper beech and monkey trees.
The old black Morris Minor is still there
and the domes of the many glass houses.
I hear the shunting of an approaching train
bringing more people home
to this safe, quiet suburb.

And just for this fifteen-minute stretch
of house-lined road and hill
there is peace on Marlborough Road to remember.
I am five years old again, opening our front door,
shocked to see your handkerchief
wave like a flag of blood on your forehead,
and to hear you call my mother's name for help,
your footprints large red accident marks
deeper than the trails left behind you
by birds on our snow-filled drive.

You were my father who growled at nurses,
*God almighty, how can a child be expected
to eat that on her own?* — when, sick
in my second year of life, nurses left me
jam sandwiches and a mug of hospital tea.
You were my father who appeared
at the top of Keem Bay, unexpected to us
as the thunder storm, with coats and hats,
umbrellas and warm rugs, pulling us safely
up the cliff edge and home to holiday beds,
wind and the gulls crying out in joy,
Abba, Abba, Abba.

You were our father
my mother watched the kitchen clock for,
climbing up the stairs at five-thirty
to make her red lips redder, her bright face brighter
just before we shouted *He's home, he's home!*
leaving behind our laundry-bin lid and kitchen-pot toys,
racing each other to open the door to you
and tell of our day's hard work —
of our tree house creations and go-cart inventions,
of the apples and pears we'd stolen from next door's garden.

I have never seen you fall since
but that day your head fell
in tiredness against the train window
just before the flash of Sandymount Strand outside,
then later fell harder onto concrete
halfway along that snowy January road.
And coming home again now, I remember how
you must have slipped, then bled, unfairly vulnerable —
and in my head I want to help you up, brush you clean.
But Marlborough Road's icy beauty keeps pulling my father down.

Poems for Breakfast

Another morning shaking us.
The young potted willow
is creased with thirst,
the cat is its purring roots.
Under our chipped window
the frail orange flowers grow.
Now the garden gate clicks.
Now footsteps on the path.
Letters fall like weather reports.
Our dog barks, his collar clinks,
he scrambles, and we follow,
stumble over Catullus, *MacUser,*
Ancient Greek for Beginners,
cold half-finished mugs of tea,
last week's clothes at the bed's edge.
Then the old stairs begin to creak.

And there are the poems for breakfast —
favourites left out on the long glass table
from one to the other the night before.
We take turns to place them there
bent open with the pepper pot,
marmalade jar, a sugar bowl —
the weight of kitchen things.
Secret gifts to wake up with,
rhythms to last the whole day long,
surprises that net the cat, the dog,
these days we wake together in —
our door forever opening.

Mint Gatherers

for Niamh Morris

While you are off gathering mint,
we stain our fingers
with a fresher smell
in the long, narrow room —
its tiny window making
four perfect purple squares
out of the far-away mountain —
that room with the yellow blanketed bed
that holds us wrapped in heat and love
over the kitchen, below the Alpine spider,
our own spindly guard
and his soft cylindrical web
in the angle of the latticed door.

The house is ours for that brief time
while you are off gathering mint
in your neighbour's field high on the hill.
You raise your hand in the afternoon heat,
rub water across your cheek, can lick already
the green coolness on the roof of your mouth —
while we, back there, taste each other.
There are no words. The lizards lie still
in the cool of the old barn. The lime tree shades
the balcony where we rise at last to stand,
now waiting for you to return,
certain you'll hang from hooks
in the kitchen ceiling
a bunch of fresh mint leaves to dry
just below where we had lain.

Snorkelling with you

for Peter

And so, beneath your things I go,
rummaging to find a pencil —
while you are still way out,
a soft seal head, curious-black
on the blue sea —
to say
what it was I saw.
How your legs moved
as though on the moon,
so slowly over under-sea ridges
that little fish came from beyond
to tickle your ankles.

Then all the day burst its shafts of light
in thin yellow slants through
the tip of the whirling blue,
as I left you behind
and approached
the arc between sea and sky.
And light looked suddenly cut
like hexagonal jigsaw pieces —
and the top of the ocean
holding up bubbles and foam
was a hammock,
weighed down with heavy things,
tied to the sky's strong branches.

All of this was there,
reminding me
that I was human and would rise again
to see the beach's rock glistening

and on it
the small gold and turquoise bird
I last saw before going below,
still there,
shaking his long beak wisely,
as if to say to me,
Go under again, go under again —
now you have found it, go under,
for there is the magic you need.

St Patrick's Day

There are moments of happiness:
me putting on Bob Dylan
to surprise you —
... *I'd be sad and blue*
if not for you —
an oval green bowl made greener
with hard pears piled inside,
the hum of the drying machine,
water rising
as steam from your skin,
the promise of a walk together
out along the damp streets
towards the copper dome of Rathmines,
your mouth smelling of me,
a book *Entanglements* tangled in our sheets,
its words like a child
whinging for our attention.
But our bed is another world,
ignores all calls.
We are listening to our own music
being added to the music below,
feel the floorboards shake.

And rain drips quietly, slowly outside
from the gutter above our window.
I watch it and count
the seconds before each fall,
then push your knees away
from the small of my back
and cross the white painted floor,
raise the blind to let light in,

see clearly the water's rhythm
beat from the moss-dark gable —
and beyond, over chimney-tops
and sleeping roofs, see the mountains
assured in their own life
calling us to rise, cross streets,
canals and bridges to get to them.
We have slept too long.

Master Chef

In a little while will you come and cook the chicken —
climb down our stairs under Vermeer's blue-gowned muse,
pass the four glass squares of our green front door and walk
to the kitchen through the white-washed rooms?

Will you leave the things you love — Robert Bly, Francis Ponge,
Wagner's screeching sirens, and come to look at our chicken?
I want you to pepper and lemon it, thyme it with your fingers,
fatten it with butter, press succulent rhymes under its skin

so that it is a roast of rhythms, metaphors and garlic, clever puns,
limes and lyrics, throbbing oven songs between our sky-blue presses.
The cat on the yard wall licks its lips, T-shirts on the washing line
are a stirring armless, headless screen protecting your great work.

O master cook, O my fine poet, my much loved chef, even the man
dangling from the green crane that swings over Patrick Street
pauses to inhale your culinary odours rising sweeter than the weed
he inhales before jumping to his death.

We push the kitchen window open, poetry rushing into the skies,
a plough, a Venus, a firmament of ideas! —
your hair a scribble of lines, your kiss sweet as a haiku on my cheek,
and this chicken startling the darkness into a well-fed dawn.

Emperor

While others might relax after love,
he is up and about in his boxer shorts,
watering flowers on the balcony —
not caring that it's overlooked
by a hundred city windows opposite.

Back inside, he pads barefoot
their apartment's wooden floors,
blasts Wagner's *Ride of the Valkyries,*
sucks dates, climbs up on a fold-out chair
to check on the highest shelf

Commodus's exact background
in his encyclopaedia,
before the wood beneath his feet
flips back, his toes are caught
and he shouts his pain to the waking walls.

Then he is that ancient emperor —
everybody, everything against him
and hearing the mob's gleeful roars
in the theatre where his anger rules,
he feeds her to the lions.

Short Love Poems

1. New Bridge

We move across each other's new landscape
excitedly, find ourselves on a new bridge
on a clear night walking across water
that has never been crossed before,
balance over a part of a river that has never
been looked down into before,
feel our bodies flip back and forwards
among the lazy mullets,
see the city reflected in our eyes.

2. Buzz of a Change

Gradually you are clear to me,
gradually it is easier to see your nose,
the neat half-moon cut of hair around your ear,
your soft skin surprising mine in a darkened room.
But then, how easily you offend without meaning to —
turning from me in the middle of sleep, snoring loudly
as a sequel to our love, while I am left alone imagining
that outside the sun replaces the moon
and that we wake from fitful dreams
to each other in another place,
the buzz of change vibrant between our ribs.

3. New Year, New Century

Steam rising from my skin,
the water dragging the old year with it
down the insistent plug-hole,
you lighting candles in the bathroom
too close to the curtain, too near to my toes,
your elbow and the toothbrush shelf.
This is how the next hundred years began
for me and you — celery and orange soup
still fresh on our breath, Bacall on the television
helping her ex-lover Bogart escape from prison,
you just talking, talking to me —
presents of new books waiting on our bed
and the past parading gifts of oils and lotions.

Painter at Work

for Clement McAleer

You have been painting all night.
A sea has rushed through your head,
dragged you way down under an idea
that must roll its way through your evening.
You have felt it come all day —
your eyes glazing over when others spoke,
your distracted reach for a brush
you picked up, then put down,
the time not right, just yet.

In your flat, your studio door is firmly closed
and the light under it is sharp, says, Go away!
But people come and go. The meat is roasted and eaten.
Cigarette smoke asks after you.
In your absence we play your music,
find in your notebooks ideas you sketched,
hear through the wall nothing,
though your open-laced shoes flung on the floor,
your jacket slouched on the door knob,
tell us that you're still here.

The ending is always quiet.
A picture fills a space, is with you everywhere —
balances over the kitchen work-top where you scoop
muesli into your mouth, is hung
just above bath water where you soak for ages,
unsettles the dust you forgot was thick on your bedside table,
is pinned high in the sky over streets you walk down
to your studio, your city becoming its beat
until at last you are satisfied.

You come home and this painting is a gift —
a bright sea view when someone is feeling low,
a vast landscape to arrive at when others gave up hope.
The hard work over, you can talk
freely of your day now,
mix olives with feta cheese and greens,
raise your glass,
your eyes, your heart,
to the life that will be painted again.

At Work

Isn't it better that you work
in your room
and I in mine, meeting only
for late-night korma, pizzas, noodles,
paid for with whatever we can find
at the back of sofas, on windowsills,
at the bottom of our vases and jugs
circled with the left-over green
of flowers long since dead?

Isn't it better we work
this way — alone, until we meet
not saying how differently we make
sense out of the air, fighting
our seperate devils that enter
without a key. Ruthless, drunken,
aggressive past, lies, ex-lovers,
childhood fears, tangled secrets unspoken,
all written forever in both our rooms?

We meet bleary-eyed, silent —
each knowing the other well.

Diary of a Fat Man

I am so fat now
that the woman I love
will not lie down with me —
so I make her shape in the mountains
of potato I've boiled and mashed,
feel her breasts in the dough I knead and prick,
her bread nipples rising erect at 200 degrees Celsius,
hear her noises gurgling with the bubbling
of tomato, ginger, cinnamon,
her kisses' extra sweetness oozing.

Skin, heaped spoons of créme fraiche,
eyes, sharp kiwi green,
arms, the curve of bananas, melons, fresh bread rolls,
mouth, a dazzling lemon split apart —
I am so fat now
she is all of this to me and more.
I make my bed in the sitting room,
unable to climb the stairs.
I sleep with my heavy boots on,
unable to pull them off.
Sometimes she passes by my door —
the dart of a thin shadow,
her breasts suddenly shrivelled
like avocados,
her skin rough like uncooked rice,
her eyes two empty plates pleading,
I look at you
and will never eat again.

Her voice has the rancid stench
of food left over for weeks.
She is becoming nothing —
ice-cream melted on a hot kitchen floor,
boiled water evaporating in a room.
But I make her again — my woman.
Her love among the carrots, onions,
broccoli, steak and garlic
is so heated in my thick, tasty stew
that I do not notice
her open the front door
then leave the house for good —
the smell of food
a jaded world forever clinging
to her hair, her skin and clothes.
Not hearing, I scoop, scoop,
scoop from my pot
into the biggest
bowl I can find.

Walking with an Architect

for Ray McGinley

I see things differently
when walking with you —
the footbridge over a part of the Liffey
we've never crossed before
that should have your roof design
with petal-shaped sails to keep
other walkers dry from our grey city rain,
the beauty of the old bank's edifice
kept so well we spend ages
just chatting about it by a bus stop
near Trinity College,
while the old woman with her trolley
listens, looks up and thinks of things
that never bothered her before, like
mullions, columns, pediments, pilasters.

This city is ours
to look at, inspect,
full of concrete, wood and plaster —
the thoughts of men on paper
belonging to years ago that became
sketches
of shadows and light,
the gasp of astonishment
we still see on our way
to work and home.

I see things differently
when walking with you,
when we play

our favourite city game —
we pass cathedrals, shops,
office blocks, banks,
until we stop at one tall oak door
standing as wide and high
as six twenty-foot men
side by side on Werburgh Street,
and with our fingers press
only to find it secretly open,
left carelessly so
this Friday's rush hour.

And we are suddenly inside
in the darkness
with no alarm bells ringing,
no stranger's hand
on our shoulders,
no security men
asking why.

Wondering which way to go,
we say nothing
move nowhere —
love the stillness of it all.

Somebody Has Died Close By

Somebody has died close by
in an old part of the city,
on a lane at the side of our flat —
a lane that I trudge along
every day and evening,
not noticing much.
But today somehow, the light
on the Castle windows made me look up
and I saw flowers on a drain-pipe
with notes flapping like leaves:
We'll miss you. May your soul soar.
Rest in Peace.

While you and I were sipping
late-night whiskey, banging doors
against each other's words,
or were just knotted together,
quiet in our dark sleep worlds,
somebody had died close by.
And thinking this, I felt
City Hall's windows rise
out of their gleaming walls,
their light shaped like a ghostly procession
of people I never knew
who had trudged up this lane before.
Then from the cupped hands of that moment,
gulls flung themselves far out across the sky
that had seemed small to me —
but was suddenly vast, unending.

from **To Wake to This** (2009)

For Lynda Mulvin and Daisy Revati
& Peter and Freya Sirr

Little Heart

In your folds tonight
are strawberries to wash away,
some knots of tuna
netted there
and up along
your neckline
sweet corn beads
that make
a precious chain.

In your head
the dog is barking
and the small wall clock
is gently ticking,
your tongue clicking
to its time.
Little heart
not yet hurt
beat on.

Twelve Days

Twelve days you've been gone.
My hands swell in the heat of loss;
in the heat of where you are —
the slow, soupy air of Buenos Aires — tapping
its grid system with your finger tips, you map
your way home down the long jacaranda avenues.

We hear traffic noise, a fountain, children shrieking.
Here you are a shadow in our heads, a voice lost
to our ears, a face fading on the computer screen.
How can I say what I mean, just how it really is?
The dog is nuzzling into our sheets, the smell of you
still there, and I can't dream without you. Come home.

Bird

for my mother

Whoever says the world
cannot be stilled
by a bird
has not been here
in this dark gallery,
not knelt on the late
afternoon floor
and gently pulled
paintings forward,
seen images
speeding by
like the old flick-books
we loved as children —
the head of a dead poet,
those dark shawls
of Markey's women
in the West.
Until suddenly
your world
is stilled
by this bird —
quirky, tufted thing
proud in charcoal,
flown over forty years
from studio to home
and now landed
in this city gallery.
Such faded wood
frames him,
and his cover

is such chipped
and mottled glass.
And yet your world
is stilled by this bird
that flapped from
Jan de Fouw's hand
when you were young
with your small children
and did not know how
you would make it to here
or that this bird would fly
forever in search of you,
his head flung westward,
his speckled heart beating
until there is no one or thing left
only you and this beautiful bird —
quirky, tufted being
that stills this dusty place.

To Wake to This

If we had known
we would not
have slept so long.
Mist has fought and won
its battle against the sun
and all is murky grey.
The spider's frail line blows
from the sycamore
to the cottage hedge,
while across the lane,
dew looks dense but breaks
like bubbles at a touch.
The fat brown birds
are not afraid of our steps
along the gravelled way,
of our fingers
stamping berries.
Oh purple hunger!
The baby dips
in and out of wonder,
twirling the soft air,
testing the sky
with her sounds.
Geraniums wake bedraggled
in their window beds
and yesterday's paint dries
at last on the red wooden door.
To wake to this.

Lucky

Lucky the man
who listens
to Monteverdi,
who walks
out the quiet lane
'Lamento della ninfa'
in his head and finds
the hedgerow yellow
with wild primrose,
the stones a maze
for the spider, the fields
undulating with ewes
and their soot-faced
soot-eared young.

Lucky the man who
hears the pheasant rising
high over Hunt's field
and is startled as much by it
as by the tenor
singing in soprano
the poem of a man
writing as a woman
in the seventeenth century —
contradictions
complex and beautiful
like dust-motes he sees
falling down now
through the sun's rays.

Clooncunny

How our hands swayed through
reeds today, brushing against joy —
the curlew calling us on in single file,
the others back in the cottage and us free,
marvelling at how we'd gotten this far, our voices
rising clear along the soggy path to the jetty,
the lake rippling with rudd and perch.
What comes next we can only guess,
can only wonder at where we are now,
at the top of this green, sloping field,
the quiet inside of us growing.

Gold Wallpaper

The night was ours —
young art students clambering up cathedral hills,
unafraid to force a window open, creak a door
inwards, brush cobwebs like a gasp of cold air
from our cheeks.

We were finding old houses
to make paintings in — you, a corner of shadows
to place your easel near, while I spent evenings
sketching the way starlight fell through cracked
glass and how the bone moon creaked.

Over ancient wooden floors,
ice-blue marble mantelpieces, the dusty mattresses
with the dent of those long gone still there,
the yellow light crept, a ghost across our canvases.
Old houses forgotten by all but us.

On and on we'd wander
up avenues swirling their yew tree spells,
scraping our knees and notebooks on the forbidden
chipped sills, our pencils and brushes scraping for life
while the rest of the city slept.

Until in one crumbling mansion,
your fingers touched mine and we stripped back
from the walls thick with damp, seventies swirls,
sixties floral patterns, the formal fifties lines —
and found gold.

Gold wallpaper lanterns and flowers trailing
delicate stems and light up to the shattered cherubs,
the intricate cornices, the tinkling, blackened chandeliers.
So beautiful we could not paint that night —
held hands and stared and stared.

Even now in the hush
of our own home,
in the dark of our middle years,
when you turn from me in sleep,
I reach for your skin —

gold paper falling onto me from you.

Sea Urchin

after Rachel Joynt's sculpture, 'The Mothership,' Dun Laoghaire

Summer came and we dived from the sea path
like feeding terns down onto the granite rocks —
bladderwrack, barnacles, crabs our after school prey,
our parents above, staring out over Scotsman's Bay.

We had rubber-clad feet, buckets as bags, we were cruel
and carefree, stuck sticks into the deep red anemone,
yanked sea sprats from their warm rock-pools,
pierced winkles with sewing needles and did not care.

Then from the sandy-bottomed waters the seals rose,
their sleekness a soft oil poured over our clamour,
and we were soothed into stillness, perched ourselves
close to the cormorants drying their outstretched feathers.

Now just there, across the path, silver droplets stream
from the sculptor's shell — a bronze-cast sea urchin turned
on its bumpy side, like an ear hoarding the sea's roar,
a cave full of children's cries, echoes of what we were

before St Michael's church burnt to the ground,
the great black birds had all flown south, the baths
grown derelict — before we ever knew the bogeyman
might come, to chase us home along the metals.

* The Metals was an old railway line built in the 19th Century to bring granite
from Dalkey Quarry to build the pier in Dun Laoghaire.

Postcard

for Peter Porter

You have been to Norfolk
and Hampshire —
then Pays de Cathare
near Carcassonne.

How odd that massacres
eight hundred years old
are now tourist themes!

You are on a train
northeast of Toulouse,
your day dwarfed
by Albi's cathedral.
Now your heart
is the flamboyant south portal,
you feel light as the lace rood screen,
your thoughts are a nave
of enormous proportions,
each second an abundance of frippery —
then Eve, like love, tugs you
to the central door.

Outside, there is the river,
the covered passages,
the little square,
the road to Cordes —
and your postcard
beating upwards like a bird
with its wings spread north.

Strange Things in Strange Places

for the sculptor Janet Mullarney, Magione Tower, Umbria

Go up the tower steps and find
strange things in strange places —
your red dog, old devil, clawing
a space on a crocheted shawl
high over the first stone floor,
knee-high blue men standing
in a row, who welcome beasts
and birds on their shoulders —
their skulls knots of creatures
jutting out towards the magic sun
and battlements of Magione.

The head of another beast
sticks out from the side of a bell jar,
nudges us down and out to a still night.
We stand high over the red-roofed town,
the cypress trees and ridged brown land.
Our giant shadows flap from the light
of the tower to its top tiny window,
then they clamber back inside, leaving
our real selves, bereft of strange things,
stumbling down alleys to a meal
where the host will never come.

Notebook Shop

All the poems we might write,
gather here in these blank books
made from vellum, soft Indian paper,
shelved in the corner shop on Francis Street.
But then a wind blows the door open,
the bell rings, and our thoughts float
out and up past the antique shops,
the Tivoli Theatre pounding its heart
of rehearsals, Oxfam's sofa graveyard
and the man from the Coombe
clattering by with his horse and cart —
our unmade poems coming alive,
flapping on the seagulls wings,
peeping into the cages of Marsh's library,
singing with St Patrick's choir,
lying down in St Werburghs
with Edward Fitzgerald and Major Sirr.
There is no end to where our poems go —
anywhere to be free, not to be trapped
in these fine and beautiful books
that are hungry for a scribble,
a dream, the rush of a word.

The Page Within

We write for the page within,
the unexpected beat
like the baby's trace
in the hospital today —
spidery mountains squirming
free of the monitor
with each speedy thump
of the heart inside,
fluid roaring like elephants
or the whirl of water all around
when snorkelling deep, deep down.

We write for all these things
and later, the slow, stiff recovery,
foolishly small-stepping
behind the mad-cap dog's ways,
every gate post, street lamp
his to make his own.
Even the glass from a car
smashed by thugs on Carlisle Street
is last night's treasure to sniff at
in the blue evening light.
And the baby ripples within
pools of my safe, sweet water —
and this page that fills, filling fast.

Night Guard

When I get home you are upstairs,
standing on the landing,
your huge book
a block of pale corn-light
wedged between your fingers,
your eyes squinting in the gloom,
your mind so fixed on Borges' words
that you don't hear me there at all,
breathing close to the turn of the stairs,
watching how it must be sometimes
when I am away from you and her.

It is late and you shoulder presses
into the frame of her nursery door
as though holding it solidly in place,
your hip like a firm nail in its side.
One socked foot presses on the other
casually, yet I know you would easily
jump into action if needed
because you are her night guard.
Intense reader but alert to every breath,
each restless move, all her tiny cries,
those early fears that populate the dark.

She has curled herself into a drowsy ball,
her fists tight under her hot belly,
one side of her face
gone pink in the furious stream of sleep,
turned away from the day she's left behind
dishevelled, well-worn, like her minute clothes
flung on the creaking floor.

Up on her wall the clock-fairy dreams
on a bed of strawberries and, from where I am,
time can be heard *ticking* and *tocking* and then
becoming your loyal pulse that beats just for her.

Magpie

The day builds itself piece by piece;
the newt joins the owl, then the porcupine,
quince on its branch bends over a ruby ring,
colour seeping across the living room floor

until the jigsaw's yacht sails to its zebra end
and we go walking, your hand a small ball
in my palm poised to roll where adventure lies,
hidden in parks, wild gardens, up doorsteps, behind pots.

Your eyes, beady berries on Raymond Street's trees,
see everything — and then, just there, *muck-pie,*
muck-pie, you call to the bird that tussles
with the daffodils, that pecks for sparkling light

like diamonds through the railings. Our day
building and renewing will not stop.
Blueberries devoured, cod stew and sleep
the warm milk of waking, later the afternoon

becoming a city of wooden blocks up to the ceiling —
only the great moon in the sky and the twinkling star
will drag you in song from your industry.
Then night has you nestling close to my neck,

your lips whispering the day's things softly.
Muck-pie, muck-pie, your little fingers pulling
at the jade on my chain feel relentless to me
like the jay all ready to steal and fly away.

Game

Into your sleep you fall.
I would go with you if I could,
where there is only your world —
a mother, a father, a dog,
a terraced house with a door
green as the holly tree that guards it,
a yard paved with our journey to here.
Jasmine and lavender catch
in the wheels of a bicycle,
a pram, or in the speedy twist
of your curious little hand,
a snail is relentless joy to hold,
a fallen branch is a wand of spells,
the door opens to us lounging
on sheets of cotton, the bed
forever blue as your eyes now
staring into mine unblinking.
'It's a game,' you say, 'I've won.'
My eyes closing, then opening to you.

Trees that Lead to You

Sycamore, copper beech, oak,
steadfast on Adelaide Road
one winter afternoon —
these trees that lead to you

flinging your day into my arms,
your face at last close to mine,
the hour before tea and the night
that sneaks you away from me again.

In your bag, a hand-made mask
burns orange as the toppling sun,
hours from me are grazed on your knees
and your shirt is a messy testament to fun.

At the steps of the church the rector
pins his dream to the notice-board.
We stand beneath these trees.
Fear not. Only love can lead to you.

First Words

Tongue on her palette
and a horse gallops
into the room,
then a story cat
leaps from her mouth,
meow, meow, meow
breakfast jam smudges
on the page
and a morning bird
is a tweet on her lips.
We hear rain, *shhh …*
see a tumble of her fingers
down to the Marakech rug.
There's *Oh deah,* when things scatter,
clatter, fall apart at her wild touch,
mwah is a wide, moist mouth
open on our cheeks
at the end of the day,
oh a plate piled
with steaming supper.
Even in sleep
she still practices.
We tiptoe down stairs,
hear through the night monitor
whispers start up again —
meow, ssh, deah, mwah —
secret lullabies from her to us.

War

Because the world
is quiet here,
because you nod
your head in sleep,
because I can turn you over,
place another blanket
across your midriff,
because the moth lands
on our oatmeal carpet
and is still in darkness,
because the wind howls
but there are no gunshots,
because we do not have to
cross borders
to a new, raw life,
or run out of fingers
to count our dead —
because of all these things
we know we are lucky
to rest here in our home,
the others, not forgotten,
their bodies battered,
their bloodied noses
barely touching.

Blessing

for Revati

To be kind —
to delve deep into the hearts
of those you despise
and find there the majesty of trees.

To be patient
with fear —
it will leave you
and you will be brave,

a child letting go
of its father's hand,
a bird cupped into the air
free …

To love life
and be loved — because
the lived life is the loved life
and so, love everything —

urban fox racing
up Montague Street,
perfect umbrella of leaves
shading a city yard
the month of your birth,
the way light falls
on your mother's face
when she sees you
for the first time …

You are just newborn,
your hair is a cloak
of dark sea-birds,
your legs tall rowan trees,
your mouth a cluster
of red berries.

You have come into this earth,
a warm bundle of things we've forgotten.
Kindness, patience, courage
blesses us and you.

May your life be lived and loved.

Postcards

1.
Waking knotted together in sleep
we unwind one another —
threads freed into the day.

2.
In her hair I smell
my own childhood —
waft of a long ago Summer
on a cold February night.

3.
When you cry out *Meow, Meow,*
after dark and only the clock ticks,
and the monitor sounds like a sea
in our room, are you dreaming of cats?

4.
Swallows break into the cold blue —
three perfect forks over The Sacred Heart
cased in glass at the top of O'Connell Street —
then cluster together, make for another time.

5.
After sleep,
you in my widening arms.
I waited for you,
I listened for you,
We are here.

New Poems

Borrowed Space

for Jenny, Chris and Anna Rose

So much happens
in this still house.
Sit a moment

and listen;
from the lavender,
the bell-shaped whites

and green bamboos
a boisterous fly
comes in —

commands the skylight,
the child's seahorses,
and paint-blown butterfly —

buzzes at last
through an open door
down the street

where our home's
noisy ways
banished me here,

away from all that clamour,
to watch rain pour down
its secrets like soft walls

for night to clamber over,
or for the fly to brush against.
Then listen; the wooden chair

scrapes back on the slate tiles,
the keys clink up from the table,
the front door's pulled behind,

the alarm instructs a tonal *away* —
the rain stops and the bees return,
this house rejoicing in an arc of light

reclaiming itself. *Hush … hush …*
its true owners are coming
nearer, nearer to home.

Gardens, Royal Hospital Kilmainham

for Peter

In the gardens people come and go
but you remain, forever striking out
from gravelled paths in white light,
from the sculptor's monsters rising
out of the fountain's pool like mud,
or from children throwing wishes,
fervent pebbles into the water.

You strike out, not afraid to leave
behind the hedges cut like cones,
the perfect line of tall green trees,
the pretty turreted house and walls,
not afraid to go beyond the garden
where the muddied path twists on
left by circus tents at the year's end.

Here the wild hill rolls our secrets
down to the old knotted tree, here
traffic roars like a tragic wind and
the old dead soldiers shift in their
graves — here you dive like a bird
into the brutal dark, then emerge
to float on the sun's waves.

Poet

The man her little feet kicked against
(fruit juice spilling across his shirt),

the man who curses, fumbles for tissues,
dabs his finger on the stain that spreads

and deepens, his shame turned suddenly
public under those harsh theatre lights,

is not the same man who, minutes later,
is called to stand and read his poems —

all fluttering in rhyme from a mouth
half-cupped by a thinker's hand.

But his words, wise as his darting eyes,
are drowned out now by his other self

who crashes against chairs, stumbles
to the exit, makes for the unforgiving dark.

Species

When Darwin's daughter
died, you must have thought
of your own, pushed your head
back against the sofa and cried
quiet tears, the rims of your eyes
turning a strange pomegranate
red while the film played on.

Then I understood that though
there have been other griefs,
this was the first I had ever
spied you trapped in, grappling
for a meaning to pull out,
rearing your face away from mine
like some sickened creature but
determined to push on.

Unveiling

In memory of Michael Hartnett

In the market place today
a crowd of writers, councillors,
townspeople, schoolmates,
gather to remember you.
How you never fell out
with your best friend,
always made him laugh.
Yes, I'm small — but perfect.

A poet rises to unveil you,
whispers in your ear —
oh, standing army of two —
then, like a magician, flicks
the scarlet cloak aside.
Now you're sturdy on a base
of stone, a glacial erratic
just landed in Newcastle West.
You're taller for posterity
and yet we're pleased;
how your hand forks your chin,
the way you always used to do
when deep in thought. And look!
You clutch *A Necklace of Wrens*.

Poet, whose head held a galaxy,
how clearly we see you now,
one foot placed at the edge
of this rock — ready to jump,
to leave the ceremony
of the market place,

to take off at your ease
down Maiden Street again.

*At Éigse Hartnett Festival, Newcastle West, Co Limerick, in 2011, a
sculpture of the late poet Michael Hartnett by Rory Breslin was unveiled by the
poet Paul Durcan.*

Julius Caesar had a Pet Giraffe

This is where the life begins —
the bicycle flung against jasmine,
the rain-swollen door pushed inwards,
dust flakes twirling in the yellow light,
the house gone still after the morning rush,
breakfast bowls thick with globs of milky oats,
the child's quiz book demanding on the table.
Julius Caesar had a pet giraffe. True or False?

This is where the life begins —
the wooden stairs turning its familiar turn,
the upper door creaking as it's always done,
the desk waiting for what might come alive
from the books, from yesterday's scribbles
like fallen hair strands on the white board.
And there's the old debris of work — apple butts
to bin, bitten pencils, new words to sharpen.

And the window to turn away from.
No distractions, it all starts over.
The back bends, hands hold the head,
the face rises, is reflected in the laptop screen.
Outside, somebody else's bicycle whirls by,
while in here, the tap-tap of things beginning —
a giraffe printing curious across the page,
before savaged by lions in Caesar's arena.

Derrynane

1. HALLELUJAH

Why should you not go
leaving parmesan shavings
on the oil cloth table,
the view a perfect dessert,
Cohen's *Hallelujah*
a victory march
down the gravelled lane,
and every breath you draw
your own hallelujah —
the child washing barnacles
from this morning's beach,
the frail bird still singing
on the electricity wire,
late Spring bees
braving the chill,
waking the kestrel
in his nest over the porch,
the pine marten in the roof.
Why should you not go?

Your whole life
is left behind.
It watches you
from the wide windows,
it seeks a home
in the spider's web
nestled in the old chair's back,
it dreams away
in the attic's high bed.

And now, see how your life
welcomes you back again,
your cheeks raw
from the walk's wind,
your lungs breathing new ways,
the dog licking
the palm of your hand
that reaches for the door —
and look, you slide back
so easily, into the life
that never really left you at all.

2. RAIN

Is it right
that the rain
should claim
everything here —
the lane that heaves
to the white old house
its chipped blue sills
and flower barrow,
the sloping field of silly
red-marked sheep,
or the unlit hill-top homes
abandoned by tourists
in the wild of winter's end?

Should it claim all this?
Make new rivers flow
down the grass-fat roads,
burst the fields with a rush,
a roar — water rising

to doorsteps,
cottages turned to boats
tossed seaward like those
from the pier's edge.
Only the bird
on the wire above
safe and free, sings.

3. GIGLI AGAIN

Unexpectedly soaring out
through the glass doorway
from our cottage high on the hill —
his aria rising over the sand,

the boat house, over your shed
stuffed with books, and we raise
our faces to his voice,
a welcome shaft of light.

Then the bird on the wire
calls to us, azaleas flare
their pink command of *stay,*
the sea roaring in agreement *stay.*

But I am back with you again
on the futon in that city room
of our early days, bowls of oranges
like sweet possibilities, your fingers

pressing into mine for the first time,
our coffee breath, the dust
of notebooks on shelves —
Gigli trembling in the room.

Letter in Winter

Let the letter say this;
how snow fell
when you walked away,

how my hands ached
for the warmth
that left with you,

how no coat could replace
your arms that had flapped
around me in a shy goodbye

how no scarf could heat
my skin as your mouth did,
thick fruit flaring for a moment

against my open lips
now chapped
by the hostile wind.

And let the letter say more;
how, even in sleep, I stand
on Georges Street again

staring until you've gone,
then I roll over, turn uphill
into the relentless crowd —

and never once look back.

Escaping the City

for Lynda Mulvin and Niall McCullough

1.
The city abandoned,
the countryside found

our giddiness sweet
as Red Bull downed

for the first time
and us *free.*

Who cares
about work now?

It's a file flung
out the window,

paper to litter
the hedgerows with,

a conference call
ringing on the useless wind,

a meeting
the jackdaws caw over,

a diary
for someone else to fill in.

2.
Our afternoon cheekily
sneaking past

the avenue's warnings:
No Entry Beyond This ...

The sublime grey Hall
our arrival point —

its side door
unlocked.

And how easily
we slip through,

could be guests come
to glide on the tiled floor

or twirl silk grandeur
down the staircase curves —

the vast dome above us
master of light, of everything

that is ours
for this moment

until a curious voice from
the billiards room: *Can I help you?*

Then evening's a hasty net
of apologies to fall into

and we scatter like sheep
over the land.

3.
Something shifts and we find ourselves
lost from each other in the same field

considering for a moment,
our own thoughts — there's a castle

to stare at, thistles piercing
our ankles in the high, rough grass

and a passage grave found for us
to tunnel into the expectant dark.

Far off, the beautiful house, its secrets
preserved in our camera's hoard, and there's

the surprise of a longed-for hut close by,
its burning stove, the table warmed by food,

and us gathering there, the sun
busy in its halo of reds and greys

this evening before June's solstice —
our old life abandoned, never gone back to.

Unbearable

in memory of Mick Dooley

Unbearable this light
on the South Circular Road,

unbearable the trees
that sway all green and gold

over cyclists, commuters,
the groaning buses, dogs.

Unbearable that you
should miss all this.

You shut your eyes
never to open them again,

never to walk like us
the familiar way home.

The Tao of Travel

For Catriona, after Paul Theroux's reading,
Trinity College, Dublin, May 26th, 2011

Even if only through trees,
even if only
across cobblestones
late on a bright night,
even if only   .
through Front Arch,
there is always a way out.

A young man
passing by
College Green
is talking about Vietnam,
bars on Georges Street
overflow
right onto the path
of my bicycle
and the air smells
of what's to come.

The future is bright,
the author writes
inside the flap
of the book
I've bought
for her
just a week after
her husband's died.
Four words
that I know

right now
cannot be so
for her.

But I think,
there must always be
a way out —
even if only through trees,
even if only onto these streets,
our lives elsewhere astray.

Rue Soufflot

There is light over Boulevard St Michel —
how it falls then clings, pink rain onto the cars
that make their way up Rue Soufflot —

and soon you will round the corner,
the Pantheon behind us, the gates open
to the Luxembourg Gardens below.

You will turn the corner, your leather jacket,
bereft of buttons, pulled to your chest, our attic
room abandoned on Rue Cujas and us here waiting.

Moment of crêpes, of Earl Grey expectancy,
of you at last, strolling towards us. It is the first time
all over again and the language of newness is everywhere.

Lost Angels

for Janet McLean

The gargoyle falls
from the bell tower,
wind blows slates
from the roof,

rain floods beams
over the sanctuary,
night fights its way
down the nave,

and deep behind
St Mary's pipes
these angels
rolled in dust

and tied with
the spiders' thread —
so long forgotten
but suddenly found.

Unfurl what
you have lost —
see how they wake,
fly free, paler than swans

under Baggot Street bridge
as they head for the Green
and the Liffey's flow,
then swoop over the cursed

Children of Lír that fall
in Parnell Square,
until at last they come to rest
in North Frederick Street,

the moon a halo
about their heads
hung in the blue of night,
petals of fire, the thin stems

of time caught in that moment.
Open your studio door,
unfurl what you have lost —
hear your angels sing.

A series of winged angels by Harry Clarke, discovered in 1968 behind the pipes of St Mary's Church, Haddington Road, Dublin, were restored, framed and displayed in the Millennium Wing of the National Gallery.

The News from Here ...

is that waves crash
on the yellow sands —
their grained secrets
stretching into
small pool mysteries
my feet ripple through,
startling the darting sprats.
I've a rock of soft sea moss
to sit on, my page blowing
in a breeze of thought,
while you've found a cave,
lean there — long-sighted stance,
your phone held close to your eyes —
Googling holiday things,
ferry times from Passage East,
a map of the twisting Barrow,
woodland flowers at Kilmokea,
Accuweather.com.

Then love starts up again,
it's a cry on the wind,
our child an urgent mark
hung on the salty skyline.
I abandon my book,
you close the articles
that opened at a flick —
Adrienne Rich Dead,
Eurozone Crisis Reignites,
City of Homs Shelled —
stuff the phone back
into your jeans pocket.

There are winkles to pluck,
bladderwrack balls to burst
and razor shells
to scrawl with on the sand,
before the tide comes in,
this day's three words: *We Are Here.*